A Second, a Minute, a Week with Days in It

A Book about Time

For Penelope Miller-Smith and the
students at Hainerberg Elementary.

—B.P.C.

Time:
a specific moment,
as shown in the hour,
minute, and second
on a clock or in the
day, month, and year
on a calendar

A Second, a Minute, a Week with Days in It

A Book about Time

by Brian P. Cleary

illustrated by Brian Gable

M MILLBROOK PRESS / MINNEAPOLIS

Time can be measured in seconds, in minutes, in days, or in Weeks, months, or years

by watches or calendars,

cell phones, computers,

or clocks that ticktock with their gears.

1 second is short, like the time that it takes to clap twice or hiccup or sneeze.

It's the **time** that you need
to recite "one, one thousand."
A **minute** has 60 of these.

A minute is also a unit of time, and 60 short seconds are in it.

8

To run all the bases or climb 40 stairs? These each might be done in a minute.

9

The Pledge of Allegiance 4 times in a row

or the birthday song 4 times repeated—

both would take close to a minute before the speaking or song was completed.

It takes 60 minutes to make up 1 hour.

Your lunch break might just be that long.

If you rode your bike

or you skated an **hour**,

your legs would
sure have to be strong!

See the two hands on the face of that clock in the square, way up high on the tower?

When the long one goes all the way round in a circle,

the time that has passed is 1 **hour**.

A day is a unit of 24 hours.
At midnight, a new day's begun.

HAPPY BIRTHD[A]

12:00 AM

So whether it's Monday or Wednesday or Sunday, in 24 hours, it's done.

7 straight days,
flowing one to the next

is a measure of time
called 1 week.

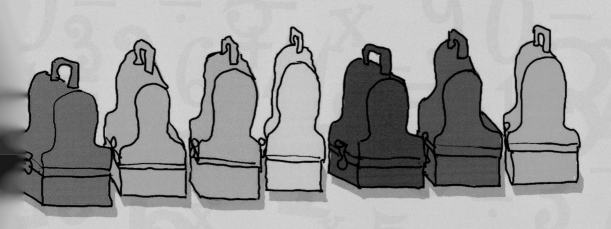

So that's 7 lunches

and 7 good-nights,

each day after day—in a streak.

A month might be 30 or 31 days, and one—February—appears

on calendars either with 28 days or 29 (every 4 years).

12 months in a row
is called 1 year of time.

And during that year,
you will handle

22

New teachers, more homework—
that's 52 weeks!—

and your cake will add
one birthday candle.

10 years as a group
is a decade of time.
A 5-year-old child will have turned

2010

15 years old
When a decade's complete!
Now let's sum up the facts
that we've learned.

A decade's 10 **years**, each with 52 **weeks**, each **week** having 7 straight days.

ONE DECADE

2010 2011 2012 2013 2014
2015 2016 2017 2018
2019

MONDAY
TUESDAY
WEDNESDAY
THURSDAY
FRIDAY
SATURDAY
SUNDAY

These **days** are each made up of 24 *hours*

of sleeping

and schoolwork and play.

that there's 60 seconds, and—
I'd explain more,
but it seems that I've run out of time!

So how do we measure time?
Do you know?

60 minutes

January

Su	Mo	Tu	We	Th	Fr	Sa
		1	2	3	4	5
6	7	8	9	10	11	12
13	14	15	16	17	18	19
20	21	22	23	24	25	26
27	28	29	30	31		

Febr

Find activities, games, and more at
www.brianpcleary.com

ABOUT THE AUTHOR & ILLUSTRATOR

BRIAN P. CLEARY is the author of the best-selling Words Are CATegorical® series as well as the Math Is CATegorical®, Food Is CATegorical™, Animal Groups Are CATegorical™, Adventures in Memory™, and Sounds Like Reading® series. He has also written *Do You Know Dewey? Exploring the Dewey Decimal System, Six Sheep Sip Thick Shakes: And Other Tricky Tongue Twisters*, and several other books. Mr. Cleary lives in Cleveland, Ohio.

BRIAN GABLE is the illustrator of many Words Are CATegorical® books and the Math Is CATegorical® series. Mr. Gable also works as a political cartoonist for the *Globe and Mail* newspaper in Toronto, Canada.

Millbrook Press
A division of Lerner Publishing Group, Inc.
241 First Avenue North
Minneapolis, MN 55401 U.S.A.

Website address: www.lernerbooks.com

Main body text set in RandumTEMP 35/48.
Typeface provided by House Industries.

Library of Congress Cataloging-in-Publication Data

Cleary, Brian P., 1959—
    A second, a minute, a week with days in it : a book about time / by Brian P. Cleary ; illustrated by Brian Gable.
        pages   cm. — (Math is categorical)
    ISBN 978—0—8225—7883—3 (lib. bdg. : alk. paper)
    ISBN 978—1—4677—1703—8 (eBook)
    1. Time—Juvenile literature. 2. Time measurements—Juvenile literature. 3. Calendar—Juvenile literature. I. Gable, Brian, 1949— illustrator. II. Title.
    QB209.5.C585 2013
    529—dc23
                                                            2012048864

Manufactured in the United States of America
1 — PP — 7/15/13